eyeseen: insights outward

eyeseen: insights outward

r.c. glenn

Big Drum Press
Chapel Hill, North Carolina

Library of Congress Catalog Card Number: 99-73173
ISBN: 1-890349-39-9 (paperback)
First Edition
Printed in the United States of America

Cover Art by Andre Leon Gray
Acknowledgements appear on page 109

Big Drum Press
Post Office Box 2406
Chapel Hill, North Carolina 27515-2406

omo'spome

the sky is very blue.
it is winded
the sky is like blue on my shirt
the sun is sh[I]ning
it is a beatuyful day.
the sun is like yellow on my pants.
the flower is pretty.
flowers are growing.
flowers are pretty.
they bloom in the spring
the grass is like you have never
seen.

contents

miscellaneous blues

miscellaneous blues

blues.   blue. is you blue?   you...

is blue!   you is the blues.   i write

you.   you is the blues.
blackisblueblackisblueblackisblueisblack
asyouisblueisblackisblackisblues
is jazz. is blues.   is rock.   is roll.

blues is not blueeyed souls
(except janis & stevie ray)

blues.   kinda blue.bluemoon.bluenotes
(haroldmelvinbluenotes)   bluetranes.

otis.   phyllis and lady sings that.
it's skatted.   transbluesency. bluesology.
blue wurld order.
            it's king b.b.   it's bobby bland blue

it's indelible blue tinting of cottoncandied lips. and blueberry
pied dentures. and bluedini koolaid gums.
and ghetto nowalater blued tongue tainter. everlasting indigo
gobstopper. baby blue italian iceconed.bluehuedkrishna. cakric
resonance.   you is my blue. you bee sound of my roy gee eye
vee.blue marbles.   play with you under
boy in blue searchlight.   i bask in your being.

bluelightbulb. squeeze you tightly between my cheeks.
crush you.
crackyou.
bluestar ointment on my blueballs.

you is the blues.

blues.
you is the blues.

blues.blackisblueblackisbluesblackisblueisblackisbluesisblacksis-
blueisblueisblackisblueisblackisbluesisblueisblackisblue is
you.

this pome

this is the poem where eye won't remind you/myself
how blk. you is/we are
this is the poem where i won't speak about your mind/
my mind/our mind.
this is the poem where i will not say
knowledge/culture/afrika.
i won't point a finger or chastise anyone.
i won't make plays on race cards.
(i'm not that good at that game)
colours are unimportant at this time.
facial characteristics. curl of hair...
genotypes are irrelevant. this time it is about conceptualization
and principalities.
(but i won't talk about that)
this is the poem where i will not remind you/myself
of how blk. you is/we are.
of how yellow you are. of how high yellow you is.
of how red you is.
("we got indian in our family?!")
of how white you are
or wannabe.
of how much green you wanna get.
(cause this is the only true issue of colour)
this is the one where i won't tell any interesting tidbits.
scream or yell. or misplace theatrics.
and poignant quotations.
i won't remind you of how phucked up things really are.
(and it's never truly all good) this poem will not contain

gratuitous jargon. sampled material. radiofriendly
rhythm bullshit balladeers. or ballads.
(over simple / predictable old school tunes)
tunes you should know but don't know. cause of pop radio. radio
won't put me in heavy rotation.
i won't have g-string clad tittybar girls dance behind me
or video shows. i won't record a record and/or bite a style on the air
or have a bulova/roley in the air for flair.
i won't lie and tell you it's all good.
and / or how phucked up things are
in this poem...
but you will remember.
cause when shit get's thick.
ancestors will remind us. it's not all good!
cause it's easy to forget...especially for ya'll negroes...
but the soul knows.

the soul knows.
                        the soul knows.   your soul
knows.
                                                              the
soul knows.
                                    soul knows.
                                    soul knows

soul   knows

  soul

                                                    knows

for romance poets to ponder true implications of overuse of expressionistic simpleton teachings

(of material love)

16 and if any man's seed of copulation go out from him, then he shall wash all his flesh in water, and be unclean 'til the even.
17 and every,garment,and every skin, where on is the seed of copulation, shall be washed with water and be unclean until the even.
18 the woman also with whom man shall lie...   leviticus 15:16-18

(deadicated to all ya'll wanna be larenztate lovejones lovepomes greasy nia longdong mofos)
ya'll think ya'll be doing some phugking.
ya'll so called poets be phuggingup.
ya'll cunt crutch poets. using cock to block the fact that your lyrics lack.
ya'll phugking fraudulent poets. ya'll think ya'll really be doing some phucking...
ya'll really be phucking up.
prepubescent wetdream poems.
adolescent analplug teen pseudo quiz bowl poets.
jiz filled heads up your own egotistical asses. ah!? ah!?   aaaaaH!?
         silly...
buttfucking for safesex.   nonlubricant latex   laidtext.
clit licking scriptures for young adult chorus fondling candleboy church officials.

prick popping   pyorrheaed propagandaed
pornographic priestesses.   ya'll pussy prophits.

         ya'lls pussies profet.   all twat topics. lips on slick dick poetries.

finger phucking mic fisting freeverse. your peers show false
appreciation with applause. in the back cafe like discount porn
movies rubbing
popcorn grease palming hoochies coochies. replacing tandem
pens drawn for random backseat used condums. friction burns on
mom's sofa/rug. entercoarse. feel burnt. naked on stage.
(ya'll think ya'll be doing some phucking)

revoke your pornographic pedophilic poetic licenses. on stage
bardson
with hardons. feeling burnt naked on stage. for clinic techs to
peck. stick you dickheads with qtips. stick your head over here let
us see where you coming from.
(open mic list is the petridish)

take a no. in the clinic.   test   the   pus.   the pus seen.
the pus,   see?
the pussy.   see. he she it is infected. infested. in fact they ill
communication

is communicable and detested. shonuff raw dogging it. crowd
erupts   (prematurely)
in phake orgasms.
giving me the sweetest taboo. kci jojo   however
you want it   however
you feel.   your making it hard for me. (ooh it's almost like
we sexing)   somebody sleeping in my bed.   your body all
over my body   baudelaires.
between the sticky sheets. pages   stucktogether.   "do
your homework!" examine the extent of impotent dicks on

petridish. what if the weight of your sperm were thought? what
if the weight of your thought were spurm? could you fillup a
cup?
"don't spillit!"
a hot body for the night. to anesthesize life.
an anesthetic quickie phuckfix in the midst of a 9 to 5 gig/shift.
phakephucksphaces stuck in chakras one and twos.
wanted: tasty smo'res who'res looking for witless zooloos up the
'ole wazoo.
your saffronic pissyellow garbs.

golden showered kundalinis.
starved for cunning language.
compositions of cunninglingus.
singus a simple song.
sexually transmitted.
my transmissions
transitions spiritually
zen transcendentalisms.
upanishads for bhagavad gita readers.
trysexuals.   buysexuals
but can't afford that.
shiva vishnu issues. hibiscus. kama sutric.
worship my paragraph phallic as obelisk. instead of common
sickness. cliched on stage. and CeeDisk. raw clitted on compact
diskettes downloads off internets.
open your mind not your loins & your pomes will follow.
not rowman. can't be roeman tick. my disease   spiritually
transmitted. homospiritually. gets into something something

tantric. fraudulent poetics. ya'll be phucking up.
birth : idea.
bring closest to life/death to heaven/hell.
ejaculation/asphyxiation. love/lust.
signifying/lying on they dicks.
long dick eunuchs. phakephucks. 12 inch vibrating realistic
blowup doll banging. closest thing to death or deity. expanse of
spurm. ovulate. lifeblood. waste. closest thing to death us
suffocates. eargasms…eargasms. orgasms or chasms?… work related
stress. a quickie phuckfix in the midst of a 9 to 5 gig/shift. is
anesthetic. imagine the orgasms you could have if you had your
freedom. imagine the orgasms if you had your freedom. imagine
the orgasms if you had freedom. imagine orgasms if freedom.
imagine orgasms freedom. imagine
                    freedome.

how much does this art shit pay?

she ask:
"so what do you do in the real world?"
i said:
"what the phuck do you mean, this is my world!?"

1.

really...do it cost?

how much do this weigh if it had said weight?
this art shit is me   it is circular /it has motion/ it has hue /
angle

and range it has brushstroke emotion   it is image and
sound and composition   weightlessness of spirits
heaviness

of fine metallurgy   it's priceless. mama where else should i
be? what could i do? where else should i go?   is there a
price

by weight of my soul and it's concept?   can the mass measure
that?

2.

we the few the starved. those that call themselves arteest'. do this
when none see. when none complement. when none critique.

when none even know.   we who sacrifice make bright for
spectator and patrone.   what if none of this to enjoy?
spectator/patrone?   we who sacrifice so that so.this is
not art on the side.

we are it.   our career orient.   even

when none compliment.   9–5 with benefit

(mama if not me   what would i be?)

how much do this art shit pay?
                        how much does this art shit weigh?

ingrates benefit.

rewards to the thankless.
                        appreciation posthumously.

why i can't dig palechicks?

my highskool peers...cheerleaders the beautiful
brunetted/blonded. buxomed thickness. in they thighs and the
brothers was like.

"she phat like a blk. gal!"   *"it's all pink*
inside!"
"can't tell the difference in the dark!"   *"it all get's moist!"*

whole misconception. and father's daughters. daughters. of
fathers. of forefathers. confederate soldiers. secessionist w.a.s.p.
and not that i wouldn't or couldn't but can't. thank you.
can you digit?

southern lilywhite. pristine. gingham hoop skirted bonneted
womanhood on pedastal.
feathery weighted dove in windowsill. whistle her in.
the fate of emmett till.   and me
smutty handed spook fantasy. peablack eyed and despised
mandingoling. (unless i reach certain status) then money green
is the best fade cream. <u>you</u> ! shavecream complex. sprinkling of
baking flour. palesister beautiful. accessible 90210 melrose. can't
dig the whole scene.
social. 'nameen?
can you digit?

seems some pillowcase shrouded face. that; that has protected
lilywhite. womanhood on pedastal. reverberates image. standard
beauty. and echoes in
my mind. indoctrinated to want something i truly cannot have.
so i

boycott.
boycott like buslots. woolworth like boycotts. boycott like texaco.
so i boycott my own cool cooncock. recollect still. eye
racketeering. remember utter fear. for life. of eyesmeet. stepoff
sidewalk curbs. as you pass taught as child ago: "when you goes
into town, you looks down boy! don't you let them see you look
in they eyes?!"
and you wonder ponder t.v. screen. bestiality intrigue. carnal
cullured reality. at one time as a youth. pondered. wandered.
through stuck pages. penthouse maidemoiselle vogue. digging
barbarella. barbwire. boderek bolero. baywatch malibu beach
barbie. in denial of a barbeque ribbed. coarse voiced. hot
combed coarse haired mothers...others that i loved or taught to
love other than.   thyself.
"don't bring her home if she can't use your comb!"
can you dig?

digging the pale and the beautiful. 90210 melrose. loved admired
appreciated. fair features. thin lips & nostrils. nonhottentots.
flaxened lithe voiced sedative. lily lover to leave fingerprint
impressions on. denial rusty sod. stretchmarked. scratched to make
ashy. thick lipped brillo domed smutty asses.
ya dig!?

i detroit red. i othello. i imagery of (god)(rodman) false flatteries.
when turned pro. great white hope for james jones. blackjack
johnson interstate commerce fate. gene anthony ray on a fame
elevator. a bigger thomas jungle influenza.

guess who's coming to dinner?   promise not a justice thomas.
yes curious but cream not quite able to digest. and not forced
to notice difference. but past events transmit. learned along
path. unsubtlety of societal status even at lack of quality for one
will settle. a smile. a batted crystal blue. a thin lipped kiss a
flatback caress. no greasy lipped rumpshake mess in some adinkra
dress.
but beautiful. accessible. 90210 melrose. lily white gingham
hoop skirted bonneted. womanhood on pedastal.
dig?

"don't knockit til' you tryit!"
"they'll do anything!"
"it's just getting even…?"
"never say never!"

i don't know why i won't
why i don't
but i can't dig pale chicks.

"never say never niggah!"

first week rain abril

cleansings.   of pollination enriched.   goldenseal dust
sprinklings.

sun.flour.flower.
on windshields.
what is allergy to some to next is sex scent.

 what is hayfever to some is lust.musk.
terra's own.
                   and pools of curry striped water.

clouds liquid blessing is like aftermath of some climactic epic of
earthen eros.
in which bird/bee semen is rinsed.

tree jism from off branched leaf.

akin to womb(myn).   but
unlike hue /mans
hue/man's grains translucent.
hue/mins seeds industrial
synthetic

first week rain in abril.
proof of.   creations holiest.

daffodil suns smile alive with the glow.

earthwurm

who will be the spokesperson for asexual rights? adrogynous
homospirituals? transtantric? heterometaphysicals?
hermes/aphroditic transcendentalist?
self realized.   self reproductive.   samesexed servants of sages.
single celled
socio-sexual organisms?

last night i made love to myself. laid on the floor of gaea. chanted
love hymns to her in hindi. absorbed his elements. as a gift.
patterned he/she/my landscape mehndi. sponged his mineral
essence. sipped her inner nectar. dipped my silverpearl grail into
thoughts moonlit stream. made dandelion licorice ale. eucharist.
unleavened bread. pomegranate wine. dined my innerself.

last night i placed my pillar of fire into the ethereals sacred space.
her astral yoni embraced. shiva in my liquified dreams. i visuddha.
i swadhistana. geminian. mercurial. face pressed against the loins
of the sun. embraced karma opened my kama gained congress of
a sacred cow. caressed my soulshell with lavendula bathed in
water of holy eternal.

last night i made love inside my cinnamon broomed tabernacle.
amongst the pools of creme candles and scrolls. on my 99th
earthdae. they will erect an obelisk. carve a fertile statue

of jade / turquoise. milky long suckling breast. seed and spear in
one arm. erected lingam in other. omnipresence. essence of cedar
resin. placed flame against brow of my forehead. lit my chakric
incense. rose / jasminum fragrance. tasted myself. opened the
universe of my substance.

                  i omo esu. i omo osun. esubiyiesubiyi.
inookiosun.inookiosun.   am one.

wrote love letters to myself in hebraic. whispering sanskrit.
reached ra. in hekau/haiku form. used chi. went inside my
mother/father to recreate myself. born in supreme image. highest
love of the deities is to birth one's self.   i am earthwurm.

hotsmr.dae '98 julie 24: pool basking adolescents await my confirmation
(or fury in light of Ga. e–coli outbreak)

how do you shit in a public pool?
how do you shit, in a public pool? how did you shit...?
fill me in.
do you stand on the fringe. white of the ledge.
ass strategically bombered over chlorinated
water like bidet?

or do you simply shit on yourself underwater and pray that the
chlorine will cleanse you as the noxious circus pebbles tumble?

or maybe someone thought it would be cute to shit in a
sandwich bag at home...

or to pooper scoop out some toilet and dump said faecal
materiale into the moat?

did you do it when people were in?
did you sneak in after hours to perform this commoners cruddy
deed?

or...?
note: if i find you. i'll make it easier for all of us and simply kick
the shit out of you!

signed
concerned tenant

ridlin

(paraphrasing/plagiarizing a letter to teacher)

★To: Mrs. Brown   sucker!
FUCK YOU
KISS MY ASS
MOTHERFUCKER
ROCKHEAD
BASTER   (or bastard?)
SUCK MY DICK
jan 1998

*keep in mind this is scrawled on elementary notebook paper with a fatyellow no. 2 in left handed writing for a right handed person or pre-middle school penmanship.

jig. stoo
(cornbreadschitterlingsphatbacks...)

jig. stew appendix A.

now get your pots and tupperware & open your mouths so you
can hear.
write butter cornbread tread through field mudred. i read &
scripted.
masses of phatbacks and brimming pots of kosher chitlings.
collardswater. molasses and corn syrup drip from my words.
paint pictures of porkchops covered with wildonions smothered
with gravy. and i ate blackened catfish. baked trout. fried perch
and croakers.
drenched in lard. and what my mouth heard. knew it couldn'tve
been no better. tries to eat halaal. no eyes or children from the
meal ovovegan ital.
regine' you don't eat no poke' no mo'? no ma'am grandma.
jigaboostooyoo ooooh jigaboostoo. jigaboostoozyoo ooooh jigaboostoo.
writes sol food.   jigaboo stew(oooh) can you taste it? it is
upon you.   listen.
i crumble the cornbread fritters of institutional mindstates into
my potlicker. getting swolle on jam-balaya gumbo   niggerah...
my niggerettes.
i crumble institutions like yellow brittle cornbread. stab at
idsegossuperegos   like so much smoke house
poke.
then i let's it stoo baby. i let it jigaboostoo i
let's it stoo baby i let's it jigaboo stew.
cause you can't cooks sol food fast.

starts at the crack of dawn. with overbuttered hominy grits.

cholestorol hamchips in the beige nary' beans of afternoon
supper. turnip/mustard green creesy (?) salad. wild grass yard
onions with chow chow and redtinted 'cumber pickles. like
granma bea bass make. take out my teef' like granpa elvin. so i
can feel the preserves i
reserved like damson plums. peach preserves. reserve serve
observe. preserves
of sols and thoughts maneyefest
in so many dusty capped tight lidded mason jars behind the
upstairs curtain.
but what's the taste of soul when it's lost it's flavor?

***eyegumbo:**
1) an exhibition thickened with african culture
2) containing mixed media construction
3)marinated in social commentary and seasoned with
consciousness

ol' folks say this hure' jigaboo stew good for the soul. dem' say this hure' fore to
remine' you of yo'self and all. just who you is. of good ol' mother africy. great
gan'mama had tol'ded me dat ol' folks say dis all that keep dem' live' and skrong
and together in slav'ry time. sho' wishin' we had some nah. you know...for yo'
soul and all.   —luscias ross

A. tomatoes
stewed
chewed
sliced
diced
fried green
eye've seen
paste   taste
sauce   saw us
marinara   marinated
marinating   saw us
thrown at closed curtain when
heckled
thrown, when heckled
catsup   cats up
cat's upketchup
halves
pulps
puree to   sauce

B. peas
hola
holy frijoles
holy frijoles negroes
red beans
black beans
green beans
peas & rice
1.50 lunch special
blackeyed
navy
butter
snaps
peas....
porridge in the pot
canned
frozen
microwaved
negroes frijoles holy
frijoles holy
noches buenos
buenos dias
beans & disease to you too

C. okra
fried
stewed
baked
boiled
steamed   (the okra does not show it's seeds
                      through it's skin)

(savor the
succulent
seed
saved
some
from
my
slave
ship
trip)

in jambalaya
in stew
in jigaboo stoo
in gumbo
in eye gumbo

* livicated to the works of andre' leon gray

mammie

outstretched   are
her   arms.
enshrouded you all.

                                     (ingrateful bastards)
she smother you with her mammaries.

                                   (mammies mammaries)
suckled you at her breast before she
fed the fruit of her own womb.

                                     (ingrateful bastards)

mammy gave of her womb.
denied her love.
protected by use of her womb.
denied her beloved.
hardhands to lay her down.
to soothe.
to escape the thought of you.
she loved the halfbred of her womb
bred from you.
mammy loved you in spite of you.

mammy grinned away tears in spite of you.

mammy grinned away pain in spite of you.
and YOU called her mammie.

tarbaby

touch me get sticky.
get stuck in my sticky goo.
tricky tarbaby
my abyssmal jigaboo.

tarbaby. ain't got to be scared to shake my hands.
tarbaby. ain't gone drip when the sun get hot.
tarbaby. is you gone let me through the front do'.
tarbaby. ain't got to be scared for me to sit wicha'.
tarbaby. ain't gots to be scared for me to live with you.
tarbaby. promise i won't eyeball your daughters.
tarbaby. promise i won't snatch your purse.
tarbaby. ain't gots to be scared for me to drink from your fountains.
tarbaby. can i sit up front this time.
tarbaby. can i sit next to you this time.
tarbaby. can i sit up to the front this time.
tarbaby. let me set next to you.
tarbaby. ain't gots to be scared.
tarbaby. ain't gots to be.
tarbaby. ain't gots to be.
tarbaby. ain't gots to be.
tarbaby. ain't gots to be…

touch me and get sticky.

tricky bre'r tarbaby.

lickrish

hmmmh lickrish purty blackassss.   you'se the deep nite sky
avon. on the tip of a fake eyelash.   bet if i dipped you in a wash
basin in a string bag. make me some black gold. some texastea.
you give me that goldenseal feeling. arabica bean pekoe
darjeeling. drink you? indeed i would. sips of your soothing sage.
indigo inkquill sanskrit   of the printed page.   soulfood for
morosage.   lickrish. you my favorite dish blk.soopbeans
blk.eyepeas pepperedjerkwingsblackened fish.   found myself
fiending your persuasion. chinky eyed indones(ian) melanation.
shonuff.   ooohlumesome.   lickarish
mmh shonuff.
luvs me some lick – a – rish.   blk. strap molasses blk. &
mild toking
got the potcalling the kettle black
        (smoking)
under my lip like i dip snuff   (she tough nah oooowee she
shonufftuffnow)
never spit the afterjuice into a cup
        (brown sugar improv.)
(can't get enough   of that phunky stuff)(i tried i tried) can
only get you as a 20 sack   (find myself wanting to take more
than two puffs and pass)   pretty blak. ass   perty
blk.   azzzssss
cocoa thai w/euphrates eyes finest moroccan toffee richest
imported

brazilian coffee. special dark hershey unwanted blk. jellybeans an
acquired taste look like something in potting soil baste.   phunk
the barbie be my hottentot venus fertility.   let me be your
blk.ken blk.pwr.rangerblk.lightningblk.falcon blk.pantherblk.sin
        nipsyrussell wiz man of tin
your lantern boy when i enter with my pistachio/nougat
complexion 'gainst your cocopuffthighs in the somali rose
candleflicker   our mixture reminds me of snickers. lickrish. mmh
mmh mm   lick-a-rish   (your
prittyblk.azzzssss)

yams

yams. yams. yaaaamms. mmmm   mmm!
don't really know about no idahoes. old earth got me spoiled on
holiday tastes.   piping hot sweet potatoe casserole.
dessert & meal. dessert & meal. meal dessert. plate bentfilled to
rim.
dense yams. pecans. allspice. pecans. cinnamon. marshmallows.
Pecans.   cane sugared.   yams.
never thought anything could take the place. tasty piping hot
sweet potatoe pies. candied   yams.
yaaammms. mmm   mmmmm.
 expected same from you. delightfully surprised by your
(super)natural sweetness. best when out convection oven
woodstove baked in skin. smashed up. firm. burnt pumpkin red.
redmud orange.
yams. mmm mmmm yams.
pull out the good chinette we eating with hands.
yams. mmmm yams.
plastic sporks yield to the weight of divine porks i mean yams
not potted meat spams. good cooked in they skins. pull out
your hot butterknife. cut my yams out they useless foils. spread
the treasured deephued skin. dangling from sinewy roots. steam
seeps from the freshly opened. warm sweettreat. spread my
buttery cream all in and around you. heard it's healthier to eat
the skin. warm hot yamplants from the motherland. yamroots.
don't really know 'bout no russet
   idahoes   luvs'   my yams.

yams from the mudaland. yams. mmm hmm. yams. yams. mmm
hmmm yams.

squash [butternut]

squash
ohmygosh   5ive lbs of grits in a 3 lb. pot   gimme big ole hot
pots of highyellagayls in tupperware pales.   got a penny for my
thoughts.
boiling temperatures till the squash gets hot. it's squash squash
squash squash squash oh my gosh. highyellow squash thick cuts
with butter in cast iron baste for taste cumin paprika sugar
sprinkle on her onions.   tupperware silkyhaired 'luminum pans.
soft feet hands
(hairstyles like europeans fakenails done by koreans)
i want a natural blonde and cherryred raven haired freckle faced
fair lenahornography. all ya'll high yella girls ain't sadittified
let me vouch. in defense of the lemonheaded queens dreadly
afroheadly elaine b. & angie d. called granma issha(?). called
mama redboned (she coal black soul though) blk. indigineous.
see; we had indian in our family before peoples peoples peoples
peoples peoples had indian(s) in they famlee. as a clichee'
trinidad to tenessee
thick lipped camouflaged halleberry queens with a vesey prosser
ghettoceleb swing. downhome house niggah cooking
hazeleyed without the contacts
seaspray blue looking. *jasmine guy (was fly) mariah carrey (kinda
scary) left eyes (burning down the house) (you can't play with my) yo yo*
on a hiphop calendar photo. lisa bonet's cosbies tisha campbell
soup all schooldaze girls ain't wannabeez. from acorns to
zucchinis. butternut squash i dream of geenies. squash squash
squash squash squash fixed with peppers and blk. peppers and bell
peppers   and   creole cayenne   cajun   and
morton.

watermelon rinds

come on thick lipped mammy
our day is over our hands are worn
our backs are bent
from wear
come on thick lipped mammy
we going to the back shack
let me be your watermelon man
my redflesh blackseeds
and lime green striped rind intertwined
with darker green lines
come on thick lipped mammy
bite into the goodness
of my firm redflesh
suck my seeds. i want you to suckmyseed
come on thick lipped mammy succeed
don't my quench take the chap out yo' thick lips?
i heard if you swallow watermelon seeds. baby watermelons
will grow in your stomach
swallow all nine of mine. nibble
          the firmflesh of my rind let me drape my
 vines over your redmud surface
let my vines creep over your coal black essence

                                        ain't
nothing wrong
 i mean. loving watermelon and all.

vaseline

look at my consistency. clean...slick..greasy..thick...rich
petroleum.
distinct. earthen. petroleum.

rub me vigorously between your palms. now sniff me...go ahead
close your eyes...breathe deep..sniff me... yeah that's it.
now rub me around your shoulders. across your head and face.
don't i remind you of the smell of vaseline coated barettes in
your baby haired scalp. don't i remind you of once cracked
elbows. ashy scraped knees. heels. ankles. forehead shiny. this ain't
no lard rub. scent of olive oil. but this ain't mamas spit in
coldhands or crisco.
silvertopped red/green royal crown with a hemp scent holding
your moisture in...leaving the back of your thigh impressions on
school bus seats & church pews. moistening away the wht. gold
patterned ash. blackness glistening in autumnal soul
glows...medicated when you be stuffy. peers hands slip away
during childhood play. back to child days sunchafes. baby bottoms
comfort.
now look at you.   step back. ooo ooh. you done became so
godawful beautiful. you done grown so much. come on. for old
times sake.
i'll be your vaseline.
clean. rich. slick. petroleum. lubricant. clear. oily soothing black
slick between your smooth thickness. come on...for old times
sake. i be yo' vaseline. scented rose lotion just don't take the chap
out thick lips.
caress me over your every fold.
over your every crease. follicle & orifice.
be my grease shined tarbaby.   i be yo' big ol' greasy
vaseline.

the other whitemeat

something explicitly unkosher in her thickness her foul
consumption made her body bumping
thickthighed frying pan tan greasiness waistline taste swine still
hard to digest
she buttered bunnybread potted meat mayo cholesterol velveeta
cheese treetmeat pressure high off the hog
she texas pete perfumed dietary jezebel, but that's not all, baby
got back kracklin' in dillard's bbq rib sauce
could it be the hamhock honeyglaze porkloin porkchops
porkbutt honeybaked
here nor there do i consume greenegg/spams don't eat no poke
but consume her hams
fried sidemeat air freshener through townhouse sardine porkbean
mcilhenny tabasco souse
you are what you eat emphatically i pleaded no rabbinical
toucheth of such that hath bleeded
breeded by swineherd castdown castout demons needed for
headswell swolefeet 'alas semen
even contaminate god in this rat cat mate israelite hebrew alike
consummate fullness of this plate
cheweth of cud/ tusk/ wildboar teeth obsessed by derivative of
Sus Scrofa 'neath unpuritanical dressexpressed
how to eat to live   she called this living noneless
"gotta die someday...eats what i eats!" she said,
 visions of chicharrones swam in her head
understanding to get here subsisted from pigmeats
natural lustful luciferean attraction,
before her, didn't digmeat.

for a cup of coffee
(a g'boro diner tale)

"good evening ladies and gentlemen.
i understand there are a good many southerners
in the room tonight.
i know the south very well.
i spent twenty years there one night…last time
i was down south,
i walked into this restaurant
and this waitress came up to me and said
'we don't serve colored people here!'..
i said: that's allright.
i don't eat colored people,
bring me a whole fried chicken!"

—"nigger"by dick gregory

what would you do for an egg sandwich?
could you endure?
what would you do for an egg sandwich.
could you endure.
the feel of your burnt flesh underneath cigarette?
jeers.
pulled.punches.spit.kicked.
"somebody, evidently don't want us here!"
could you endure at a diner?…punched.smacked.
phlegm filled salivary strand ribbons of courage.
and kicks.   for blk. coffee and two over easy.
what would you do for a cup of blk. coffee and danish.
and two greasy overeasy & drytoast.
if a waitress said: there were no eggs…except down the back of
your
pristine blazer.
your proud pop bought(maple syrup stained)
3 inch hemmed. creased starched. school khaki's.
dripping. klinging. from horn rimmed prescriptions.
and processed wave.

can you see through. biscuit flower obscuring
view? would you still want egg sandwich?
would you want black coffee hot and scalding?
staining   fresh.   pressed white starched buttonup.
and crisp cotton tie.   given to son by proud mom.
for an egg sandwich and black coffee.
what would you do? for eggsandwich.blk. coffee.
danish. and drytoast. twogreasyovereasy
could you endure.   all for a cup of coffee?

(torchthephuckingwoolworth)

blk. folks souls

blk. folks souls sho'll got a different taste nah'

you know
the taste of tea at uncullured church socials
of
sidemeats unseasoned to taste and served
of
water basted darkmeat
the taste of brown bag
and
litmus paper chalk

they souls sho'll is a different taste than what they was nah'

shakerag buck

shakerag buck

this is the story of shakerag buck
colored cloth peddler.
patterns and polka dots and ginghams
swatches of pretty pink and lace.
patterns and swatches of baby blue handclothes
strewn to the four winds.
askew restlaid on dandelion grn. bluegrass
swatches and patterns of polkadot/gingham
cloth to buff shoes and patch holes.
corduroy and denim cloth rag peddler.
polka dot and gingham cloth rag peddler.
travel your wares.
heard a mutt got ahold of your bag buck

tsk tsk tsk

spread your rags across red mountain.
over and across moriah countryside. windblown look of cloth
leaves
shakerag buck colored cloth rags
enough to shake a stick at.
autumnal grace of stray dog graced to add
shakerag name to the places face.
sprawled across lawns like oaks shed autumn.
make the cullurd town more bright.

angelsong

we go back to places familiar
that's why they built wooded homes
and brick stone homes that absorb sound vibrates
and essence so when we return to these places it is healing
because we regain that which we have left there be it childhood
or our former more virile selves. these walls hear us. they know
us. they remember.   she sits opposite me. we both in
kerosene stove heat
slumber. not the type that is necessarily discomforting. but that
which aligns
the soul with the everpresent. i twenty five or so years removed
but still the same feel. oil heated stove. she has been the same
age for 50 years to me. right here in this rooms comfort my
deepest sleeps. and she not moving quite as fast as before but still
to me the same age as she was 50 years ago. still beautiful and
graceful in her movements. and proud. over here in this recliner
chair and her angelsong would sing almost inaudible:
without god i could do nothing / without him i would fail / without
him my life would be rugged / like a ship without a sail....
daddy always having something to say about something and she
more consuming. observing. i suppose hers the very eyes of the
universe. and ears of a galaxy. right there in that chair. with the
mt. siloam fans and great roseanne to
the back right in that same corner framed for 100s of years and
that lamp there since before the house was rebuilt by uncle buck
and paw paw
w/ the aluminum roof. addons to a once sharecropper dwelling.
she the soil and backbone strong stern and silent as mid 1900's
women. and the walls forever carry
her angelsong.

this one they call cowboy

somewhere in far off rocksborough at the local mailroom he
stands
weatherworn denim cowboy hat connie weaver gave
with the authentic multicolored headband. and a gentleman
asked:
"where are you from sir?"
who is this one they call cowboy?
this cowboy eyes of wool grey with eyes of the smell of bluegrass
and sky if the two were one. this one they call cowboy without a
horse.
and usually in liberty overhauls   and elbow
holed flannels and through his eyes of wool with the sound of
bluegrass
and the sky if it were the ground   approached roseanna
cause he seen many a thing. but he knew when he saw. a pretty
ol' fine thang named bea. silky haired thick calved honey skinned
and high cheeked cause a cowboy gotta have a ponderosa flower.
this one they call cowboy. saw pretty silky magpie haired thang.
clover hone toned dreamy deep eyed highcheeked strong calved
woman named beatrice. (cause cowboys need companionship)
beautiful dandelion flowered beatrice. i remember this one day
cowboy from the foldout sofabed. chainlight clicked to early
morn milked cows jay blue skied sharecrop land. this one they
call cowboy eyes of wool grey sight of sky blended bluegrass and
the sound of folk banjo. railroad snuff clayglaze spitoon beside t.v.
recliner. beside l.b.j. current president since the first metal
wastebasket.
no horse but a thoroughbred 71' powder blue caddy seville plate
HIS.
weatherworn denim cowboy hat with the authentic multicolored
headband grey wool eyes and he answered:
"i'm from everyplace i ever been and it won't be too long 'fore
i'm away from here!"

grammalima

remember grammalima. down bahama way.
grandpa james mama.
more like great great grandma she was.
another life it seems   i   by she greeted
in that home.
house immaculate with that greeting sniff
of grandma house.
of sweetness of redmud look to yampie.
of peppering perfect of phatbackgreasefried chicken.
white wood stove and frigidaire same
from sears catalog bought year forgotten.
time suspended of some MGM Grand
1920s something movie.
and potatoepie pan shine.
like out in garden   afearing
crows.
house frame antique standard of some era bygone but still.
seems like ages back. i am there.
behind pines that touch skies out back and pastorals to distance
infinite.
behind her home alone she. other half in spirit still move.
'mongst shadowlight in curtain and
goldrays through blinds his pictured testament to protect.
her chicken coop. outhouse recently retired.
i can see.   i remember.
house immaculate with that gramma house greeting.

buttermilk churn

and sound of something butterfried
and wonder why the taste enhanced by this room on holy land
and by hands touch of gates gold and
honeymilked hum of some ancient gospel chant
and barely a dustyboxfan breeze   cause
too much would remove   heavenscents
and sound of some static bluegrass a.m. barely
and some appalachia announcer drawl
we there every yr. round 'bout this time at grandfather or
chimney
and still not quite as breathtaking as the aroma of
hardcooked corncakes & apples on piepan servingtray
hand towel faded with recycled troutgrease
on the table something fresh
on the table something tupperwared
and we see clearly three miles downroad visitors from
screenedwindow
all underneath the incessant drone of a 911 scanner
(mama never did much like that)
see this place holy
this here is a communion bench
this here where suppeth apostles and the like
seem like
diddy at the table head
mama always to the left
she & liza afternoons bob barker   and GH
& OLTL   & AMC
plots memorized for 30 yr. or more
in the corner near the sears catalog stove stood her
buttermilk churn

luminum roof

installed with precision.
if i think hard i can remember when he by hand installed it.
with the ridges that provide unobstructed water runoff.
it was at first open to the elements except from above.
then screened in.
then i would imagine cola bottleemerald plexiglased
and extended.
i can hear it now.   voicing the silent.
listen....
raintalks so distinct on country luminum rooves.

brunswickstewpot

an orangeish brown. frayed edge. possibly polaroid
if they were out then.
	water colored polaroid of men and women.
who were infants. amberhaired infants. braids. barettes.
grinning and careless. and uncareful because the
time is not dangered.
who were infants.
and a smoke wisp scent rose from the castiron 50 gallon brew
to feed a tribe. purple long banana seated.
glittery. whitestriped seat.
ambered afroed boy infant.
and cousins surround second and third not sure of all the names.
	gathered for faded orangeish redmud brown overexposed flick.
taken back twenty or more it seems. pepsi cola
thermometer then slight
rust than now under wood shed shelter post
and dustytobacco treaded twine wrap table.
uncle archie there. and lucy & hallie i see just as clear from
chimney window.
jack w/ callie bea and mollie bespeckled. and shining. and
smiling. but only inside.
because these women are from time ago portraits
giving no indication

of their joy, they are happy yet worn like mama roseanna's hands.
and all the grown folks are babies now. in this
polaroid orangebrown.
pond background. beside cureshack. beside dog sam. beside shed.
underneath there are hay bales. beside electric cow fenced. and that
behind clothesline
and waste barrel with rust holes that fire sparked crackling to
newspaper additions. and conjure pot with meat. and corn. and
potatoe. redmud orange brunswick magic to feed an entire tribe.
under cotton billowed bluejay sun.
my kinship.

chipped paint metal sofa

chip paint surface.
refinish.
feel groove movement bumpy weathered.
green lawn chair. one white centered.
red trim.
braille his tale across bare palm.
sidegrips friendly hand worn.
weathered.
lawn or front porch placed rocker.
steel sofa.
(like what uncle brody & mr. jones gathered to)
squeaky back forth comfort.
swaying sleepy eaze of country breeze
for snooze.
oiled spoiled soothing calm.
on porch surprisingly.
orthopedic though.
chipped paint metal sofa back.
supportive cradling.
sunday funny coupon cushion.

redmud

it be blood in the mud.   it be blood in the mud.
it be blood in the mud.   that make that redmud.
that mud red.   why you think yams look
like they look.
why you think   squash   look like they look.
why ya'll think   sweet potatoes   look like
they look.
why ya'll think   corn   grow   like
they grow.
why ya'll think   collards   grow like
they grow.
it be blood in the mud.

redmud on soles.   mud
red of souls.   it be blood in the mud and sod.
soles be drenched with   laborious soils.
souls be drenched with   murderous toils.
it be lifeblood.   it be flesh.   it be death.   in the
mud confessed.
soils   souls   soles. soles   souls   soils.

soils of redmud blessed.
and lay down your burden.

to pray.   and pray that the soil shall tell the soil soles
souls.
and pray as you lay.

hope she does not open up   to speak.

john   lyons

we remember john lyons.

we remember john lyons.
might have been a johndeere. or
the red one with the IH on the nose

and greyish paint grill. softspoken. not
much at all even. same overhauls w/ work
grease evident.

dear john lyons,
we remember

you. on the red grey faced IH tractor. probably
doubling as a means of vehicular as well as sharecrops
device.'member mama and diddy giving what they had.
up on the hill. you. 3 daughters in a c.1884 shotgun shack
to you still like some castle on your hill. seem you had it all.

heard you never complain. modest as he. john lyons face
of blk. berry leafs simplicity. and he.

remembering john lyons.

punch hill store

a remnant of eras bygone.   or not so.
and snuff dust sits on daylight streams   like idle minds
from corner window.   (malignance)
quadpaned to bottle capped tiled floor.
like minds stagnant.
cocola caps litter dusted   groundlike snuffdusted. rusted caps.
snufflike dust.
bench splinters somewhat   pleasurable 'neath liberty dungarees.
and old pumps out front.
c.'43 no longer   functionable
conversation casual but abrasive
and i feel paw paw pain from tight jaw
out there moriah
passes time 'mongst
general store items too cobwebbed
and dusty for purchase
but convo.
i feel paw paw pain from tight jaw of general store.
ignoring ignorance of general statements

caleb daughters

apprehensive at this
we dined   we elvin daughters
and in the back of our mind
the pact that had been denied
by diddy
letting us handle as sole heiresses
her   skin fed this land; his   sweat quenched this land
her   hands fashioned this land; his feet carved this land
and in our hands he held it's fate
this sharecropped land filled of oursoul
diddy had told old caleb 50 yr. bk.
the plot was not to be allotted
all this which we share cropped(ed)
and til '75 owned none
'til tilled from andrew hill
and apprehensively we dined
in the back of our minds land grants and pacts
ago retract'd   (the plot?)
and on this day calebs daughters
land loot lustful grins
hoping diddy's senility had done in
asked the same   w/ no shame
and we say as he say
our soul is not to be sold

marshall mccadmey

you shouldn't oughta' pray so marshall

you shouldn't oughta' pray sucha' thang

you know how it does you so…

thus of such apocryphus marshall mccadmey prayeth.
that jesus deliver he from the hives of swine ingested.
knowing that doing so shall result in welps and
skin epidemics you have never seen since forbade leprous.
but marshall mccadmey prayeth such a thing to not
afflict for love of a thick slice of sidemeat phatback.
he loved so to detriment….

you shouldn't oughta' pray sucha' thang marshall.
you shouldn't ought to pray such…

henry gayles

easter sundae 1999 aftermeal porchtalk:

heard tell of henry gayles
when t.v. was first out
would don a shirt & tie
to be properly dressed
for visiting company;
see henry gayles hearing /
seeing the transmissions
thought since he saw them
they saw him.

good old henry gayles.

god bless him.

tobaccotown

tobaccotown

welcome. where big whigs brawl and steel.
livelihood of cashcrop that has sustained and given fame and
name now...
medicine (for a city filled with so much sickness) where urban
renewal and expansion
kills trees. trees die and industrial landscape flourish.
EE-KO-NO/Socialism. still czechs spicks jigs nips necks on the
other side of tracks.
(jesse helms reconstructionism)
seccesh confederate conservatism. is...laced fruitcake. stars and
bars
flavored with rainbow flag icing.
(neo liberalism has thrived off of previous amendments for race
baseism)
what once was green now qtr. mile obligatory minimall and BP.
once agricultural traderoads now workzone/speedzone
deathtraps.

tobaccotown. welcome. collegetown. educated:less self
introspective.
collegetowns. factories for less culturally agitated clowns.
where big whigs brawl and steal and stall livelihood of cashcrops
in fear
of joe camel and marlboro men...tainting scholastic aptitude

impaired youth.
where big whigs brawl over meyer and liggett cigs. cashcrops that
have sustained and given fame. and longstanding generations of
farmers with
no other angle choked by carpetbagger park. new prison
complex
across from new
athletic park. yankee influx like ears of corn like tobacco worm
on tobacco leaf lopped off. and john deere tractors replaced by
UPS striketrucks.
where urban renewal and expansion kills trees
a forest dies. a city grows.

                          but does it live?

mamadot

mamadee mamadot mamadee mamadot mmmh mamadee
mamadot mamadee mamadot

you so fine. i gots a crush on you. you was my first love. always
had a crush on you mama. love you so much my omo is you. i
mean. what you expect? for a little while just me and you mama.
me and you mama. me and you. mama do that liquor house
dance you useta do.

mama.

had me protected out of your sight in a den full of shewolves &
lionesses as warrior cub. taught me the ol' ways. taught me the
ways of womb. spoling me

mamadee. mamadot.

doing your thing. kept your baby boy firebrown plaits intact.
alone raised both boys.
when a biological didn't bother. frugal homecuts me and baby
bruh. now our role as older brother or jealous lover we watch as
you grooveback. love you mamadee. ain't gone let them hurt you
mamadee. ain't gone let them get to you mamadee. you too good
for this place mama. me and you mama we got our passes. we
gone fly away from here mama. just me and you. wish i could fly
us away from here mama.

mama dee.

can't find nobody mama. nobody like you. no heavenly body
down here mama. you broke the mold mama. you set the
standard mama.
too high.
mamadee mamadot mamadee mamadot mamadee mamadot

mamadee mamadot mamadee....

they just don't make 'em like ya'll no more.

charlescarreycarma

trying to build the gumption. trying to build the disdainful
stamina of deceitfulness. the gumption to build the
deceitful stamina of disdain for the untangible. trying to be...
let's see uhm. what's the word. animosity.
trying to feel a certain level of hatred(?) towards the unknown.
a chromosomal father figurine. a one halfing of a genetic mapped
figurine. eyes have never met. in mirror trying to dissect
distinctiveness. mama unexplainingly lashing out at character-
istic familiarity of character identity pickup of one i have
never laid eyes on...or have i.
a misplaced father figured. trying to develop that hatred and
reach
back to a time when manchilds inquisite fatherly presence. and
then.
a substitute acquired. universe's creator fathered and shadowed.
interjection of a lack thereof familiarity situation would part a
godchild's pairing for self concepcioun. want to be embittered for
the cubscouts and football games. want to be angry for the
missed songs sung and plays. want to lash out but can't grasp
enough negative emotion to have disdain.
"you don't know what happened between....?"
still want to hold dread for singlemom's latenight shift pay.
to support boychild. but can't grasp enough negative emotion
from lack of father figurine. for love feel the angels have cloaked.
and if incorrect cloaked in karma.
hoping whoever right or wrong.
bless you father.

bastard native raisin sun

*birds flying high you know how i feel / sun in the sky
you know how i feel....*

shadrach meshach★ look down the old country road. seen myself
coming.
redmudsoiled.
bleached babywhites. bilalian beckonings of bron and
bondoukou.
baraka's grand baby boy. held high on shoulders of rustic winds.
for all to see.
sanchez stepsun. nikki's niggah can you nephew.
richard wright's bastard native sun. lil' redmud soiled raisin in the
son.
hues of hughes. last poets last poet apprentice hooked on gil scott
heroin.
baraka's grandbaby boy held high on winds shoulders
honey suckle scented.
bastard baby bard. mama lucille's infant. mumia fruit beared books
of brooks
loins with
stevie/hathaway theme music as backdrop.

★ for phillie shabba.

blk.pwr.fst.pk.

sching..   sching...   doiing...   boiing...   ouch!
peaknaps.
peaknaps fly. beebees schiing "hold your head still boy!"
patent no. 23882   blk. pwr. fst. pk.

blk. pwr.   blk. power fist pick
tuning metal rods scrape.
dome raked "right on baby?"   through reminiscent cotton seed
separations.
black eyed peas torn into puffy burnt brwn. plummage.
peas porridge in a pot.
peas sching on the back of the neck naps.
sching   sching   sching   kitchen like
stringbean snaps.
NATCHA!
black power fist pick.
blk. pwr. fst. pwr. picking thick plastic.
handled muscled veined. flexed unseen.
tricep flexed flexor dig-it   -orum superficialis.
molded base of industried plastic.
clenched thick knuckled forearm fist. with peacesign seethru ctr.
(not to be confused with...not one of those complimentary
plastic teethed thindomed combs for picture day photos)

black power fist pick or selfsheathing grn.redfold
down handled rd.grn.blk. bodied electrical metal
receptored pronged greenblackred.
remember when even haircare meant revolution.
afro sheen afrosheen ...let your sol glo.....

probably c. '78

...in the lab sample yellow/paneled
family station wagon.

                                                        facing N.

traveling S.
on the vinyl folddown kids/pets backseat.
w/   the   panoramic   view
rear   windshield.
snacks?

probably cracker jacks in cooler.
1/2 dollar sized hambiscuits hors d'oeuvres
and cold cocola in the can

        (case one of us kids couldn't make it to the
        rest stop; shielded by the lab sample yellow/
          paneled family station wagon door)

1980hero

his name is capt. adventure
ten year old sidekick of   no one
powered by literature of john byrne x-men & fantastic four
outfitted with amfm walkie talkie helmet
bought the christmas before.
cotton zips   for quick   greek dodgeball   movements
dodging various imaginary
villains and neighborhood canines unchained with
attack postures.
skilled in dirtclog pyrotechnics specialties.
he trains while peers played unorganized games of pickup at
subdivision citypark courts.   traveling through
neighborly manicured.
lawns across trickling creeks and streams rippling.
popping wheelies
on curled   handlebarred   tasseled.
whitestriped   purple sparkled   bananaseat schwinn.
coated playing cards or cardboard in spokes for   realsound
harley putter.
uniform: handmedown letigre tightcorduroy huskysize
sears roebuck.
knees patched from gymfloor waxed sliding. by tender mother.
tender mom with innate abilities to.
mend youthful superheroes uniforms.
abilities: excellent at the toss of trashcan lidshield with thick
perm. markered insignia.
(so as not to be confused with capt. amerikkka)
battle record: only foiled once when older brother of arch
nemesis beyond adjacent backyard fence smashed amfm walkie
talkie cybernetically enhanced comm. device
meet capt. adventure!
pray for innocence of childhood lost.

royale ice cream parlor 1957★

(a true account of the first but little known organized sit-in of the (un) civil rights movement)

"we should like to have ice cream this noon!"

we thought with the anticipation of victory in mind and the taste of rocky road on our mouths. easing back to the rear swingdoor up the concrete stair where we are allowed in to the royale but are forced to be unseated in rear while 'other' patrons sit. whilst we second classed and 'others' enjoy pure import crystalline cream vanilla bean w/ the specks. us 2nd classed not yielded the commodity of a boothspace. premium icemilk on the corner of rox. & dowd in the midst of the colored comm. and we 2nd classed denied the commodity of a boothspace?

"as i remember it was very hot, about the third sunday of june or the 4th , the smr. of 1957."

 in this particular heat when caravans of icemilk lines stretch the length of mother liberties wingspan.

"we decided we should like to have ice cream today....!?"

so we ordered strawberry waffle cones so we ordered sundaes w/ nuts chocolate sauce whipcream w/ cherry tops from booth to booth we moved (despite incessant prodding to relieve our godgiven) and the manager indignant, ears and nose and neck red with ignorance on his lips never said a thing with hatred burnt in his eyes. so we

ordered malts and shakes and cocola floats. so we thought with
anticipation of victory in mind and the taste of rocky roads on
our minds. newsprinted in the memory of the curious
neighborhood children noses pressed against the parlor glass to
witness
us history. 4 cars and 8 police later. and one sitter departs and his
name in us history is forgotten

("i can't recollect that fellas name!")

 and icecream drips. and icemilk melts. but the taste of premium
rich rocky road was our taste of victory.

p.s. charles dunham got good chicken there now.

*livicated to mrs. va. wms. thank you for the insight &
pioneering.

tips for UNCullurd/STATE
students/alum/supporters dissatisfied with current cullurd affirmative action mandates

settings: gothic ivey leaved/leagued stoneworked institutions
accessories: tar/black shoe polish. jhericurl/afro/process wig.
                 white clownpaint applied 1/2 inch under nose,
1/2 inch
         from chinbottom, two inches from mouth corners to
         exentuate pickaninny fullness...
         ...a la al jolsonesque/ted danson
mission: kill your proverbial two blk. byrds (jim crows) one stone.
al jolsonesque/*c. thomas howellike (i.e. soulmanesque)

*no The Outsiders greasers please!
with darwinian precision; ace the s.a.t. prepare a concoction of
negrifying skin agents.
(see: tar/shoe polish/axle grease)
(see: most early 1900s blackface/strawhat vaudevillians for
modeling)
         pick up various ghetto idiosyncracies via cable
         i.e. springer, stooges/rascals. UPN...or study..
         blaxploitation flics circa 70ish (superflyshaftpeteywheat-
strawsweetback)
         (please, no suave ron o' roundtree lead roles!)
be careful if invited to dinner/meet/greet parents
buffer convo w/obligatory: *"did i tell you mark was attending
harvard law school....?"*
but pop hears:
"go get me some watermelon and a hypodermic needle...whitefatassslut!"
bump sam and daves soulman as often as possible for moodset.

assume some really cool ethnic identity i.e. muhammad abdul
jabbar or kareem ali.
to seal the deal, find you a half negro /anglo love interest.
(irene dawn chong)
unless you are on an 'athaletic scholarship
(please, deeper shaded love interest are strictly prohibited!)

(don't forget to smear torsoe and other extremities for gym
shower scenes and intimacy)
[WARNING! tarring and shoepolishing will not replace what a
good swedish pump will supply (careful of mandingomyth
coverblown in intimate indulgence)]
suck-it-up when you eavesdrop insults in the bookstacks, hey!
after all your not blk.:
Q:"why did the negroe wear a tux to his vasectomy?"
A: "if i'm gonna be impotent, i want to look impotent!"
arbitrary chastisement by blk. faculty figures will show that no
favoritism towards minority students will be tolerated.
[also periodic random i.d. checks/vehicle searches will be
performed to show you are
black like me.]
see: book titled same
all this will insure you break the color barrier

good willie hunting.

NOTE: all quotations courtesy of (comedy?) SOULMAN
starring
c. thomas howell

where will the negroes go?
for j.h.f.,j.c.& h.w.l.l.

underfundedunderattendedunattendedunaccreditedunappreciated

shame on you blk. mammy blk. pappy your alma mater ain't good
enough for your daughters? shame on you blk. mama and papa.
same school that you. first generation
college student stood so proud of. sharecropping granmammy
granpappy help send them . so proud. had chance to go. now you
shamed to send your sons.

                                                             shame on you.
under-   un-   none-
                                                        -attendance
you. dubois' talented tenth attend cause this your favorite t.v.
team since you was in the 'lebumth (11) grade. built brick by
brick exenslaved hands and ideals.
training schools seminaries (never meant to be) state legislatures
misallocate underfund
close and quotaed. no need to allocate funds purpose served..
somebody told you the
paperweighed differently. hide your blk. speck in kegthrongs
won't erase you. hide in the bonfire herd. take the bass out of
your speech your smutface can't escape. you a niggah that's all
you ever gone be. a thickskulled niggah...least in they eyes. token
spokesman of your cullurdmen. your action affirm has misplaced
his anglokin.

bcc centers for revolution fronts in the six-o's. nine-o's: blk.
student   move
yourself off that ingrate campus. since 58'   and you still
trying to integrate.
(you ever noticed how silly summa cum and magna cum sound?)
state legislate   they play reverse quota numbers game:
                    you.
full course load/fulltime job/scholarship/partial. majority now
minority/tuition in full?   nonattendance.
unattended.   underattended.   underfunded.
                            but where will the negroes
go?
unappreciated because you that's there is unaware. in the last
bastions of historic
negritude/intellegentsia. trapped in your fratbraggings and
videofashions. complain daily about administrations. lunchroom
vocations. homecomings. who playing?
negroes, where else we got to go?
anti-cultural/socio spooks that s.a.t. by the do'
to a negroe church commune with yourselves
to a negroe family reunion commune with yourselves
to a negroe community commune with yourselves
to a negroe school
            commune with yourself!

but go ahead. give it away like you did boogie woogie. like you
did beebop. like you did blues for fascimile suede shoes. give it
away like you did your a.m.e. baptist church pews. scour the

agriculturalist with elitist views. everything got a price especially
your souls. like neighborhoods and harlem south avenues. tell
family business like nappy
jheri bags in news.   ignorant ass blk. athletes
in interviews.
you some   blk. bull connor.
you some   jigaboo   george   wallace.
you inadvertently close the doors of ncc's, 'skeegees and fam-u's.
crack the pillars of
howards hamptons and c.a.u's. chain the entrances of livingstones,
lincoln's and prairie views & fisk. forsake self for facilities not
long ago denied at ole missbama's and echoed going back to cali.
on a 209.

that's right. give it away when you live for your negroe college
homecomings in jetebonies.   next year the show will be
hootie and crowned queen yasmine bleeth.
then   where will the negroes go?
"…but fuckit, could never learn a niggah nothing noway!"

uncle sambo

intro to jigkus (jikus)

do voodoo:

...spread cemetery dust.
and chicken bones.
make voodoo dolls.
of the enemy.
(stick
them
w/
pens.)

justine & libby

"oh say can you mufuphucking see, by the dawns early
mufuphucking light?"
—fontaine

will you go with me? check.   yes ☐
no ☐
come on babysodomize me...
beatme... chainme...handcuffme...
i admired her.wanted to be just like her. and she...
carried a flame for me.
it burnt me. it burned me. it's burning.within her
womb(firenexttime)
burning.   burning.

burning.
experiments left my groins full of napalm
burning. (agentorange)(tuskegee)
(gulfwarsyndrome)
(sscrematoriums)
my deeply committed love jones. loveded. blinded.
she left me with cargohold soiled sheets.
same ones she drapes her harlotry.
same ones she drapes over her sons heads.
i'm   burning~~~~~~~
libbies love for unusual mango(strangefruit)
on trees. watersports fetish(firehosewaltz)
bondage(picnigs) and fiery things(lawncross)(churchbombs)
left me to burn.
demasculinized. penis envied.

socio/   spirituo/physico/ castrated.
         u.n.'s very own eunuch.(the statue of liberties a prostitute)
that's right   a whore   a harlot   a trick   a stunt
                                                                a tramp
                  a beeyotch. and i'm a john named jim crow.
                          wanting to be her queen i hoovered.
                                    crossdressed. blk.list.
          to infiltrate her. touch an orgasmal nerve within her.
          her village people fantasy soldier boy in olive fatigues.
          thought it would get me over deeply committed to her.
                           sought self ass- simulation.
          my blk. ass being the pimp that i am or often portrayed
                          kicked my patois to her at the bar(assoc.)
                  she referred me to her freaky-er twin justine.
                          she was only 14(amen)(dement)
      stuck on '69 and before. see how they likes to menage de' trois?
      (just you and them) the statue of liberties a prostitute. " "
                          see justine fiend the sado- scene.
                                ways to enhance her p.i. see?
                  she pack a colorblind fold to the fact of my mack.
                  made an indecent proposal two hundred and nine.
                  she puts me on lockdown. upriver anal plugs.
upnorth nipple rings.   scrotum clamps
                          intact(hamstering)(freakything)
      C. I.   ain't useta being cranked crunk and smack and crack
                  and junk pumped into my innercity blues
                          had to find a way to support my habit.
pimped my mental . naive and gentle so they experiments on my
                                                            genitals.

artificially insemminated baby sis.
unjudicially incarcerated baby bro.
mammy image never menstruated.
pappy image never educated.
boob tube put us on w.i.c. in someones school/poli sci fair
project
reinterpreted. our values family. some say her nephew
(justa)(mr.) bill did not inhale.cigar stale.taste of tail make you
not wait to exhale.
left hot air when apologize for free syphilli.
in place of some earned justice. the statue of liberties a prostitute.
starting to see right through you starting to not like you.
whore. bitch. stunt. cunt. twat. slut.   freak. harlot.
trick. start to understand.
why sam's misogynist.
see she ate me out. i mean she ate me up. she ate us out.
see: Amerikkka eats her young.
her prisons are school systems. her school systems are prisons.
(las sistemas escuela son prisiones.las prisiones son sistemas
escuela)
her prisons are bellies of her bestiality. (prisoner polity reality)
rubberwombs filled with botched abortion.
rendered unbarren unproductive unpermitted growth.
and repeatedly (without fail)
but unsuckcessfully. (she has tried to) (clothes hangering)
resorting to swallowing the jiz of ancient kush.

doucheme a melange. a multicultural medicated melting
pot...boiling over on the supreme court floor.
see: you is the real pmp.daddy. used me. now don't need me.
don't love me no more. abused me. now that i know what i
know. can't love you no more. whore.
found the electric prick you used to do me in.
under your robes (hermaphroslut)
no telling how many others you done phucked.

the statue of liberties a prostitute. the statue of
liberties a prostitute. " " " " " " " " "   "

when they bombs baghdad

did ya'll know that babies get burnt that
babies get burnt that babies get burnt

that babies get burnt that babies get burnt
that babies get burnt that babies get

burnt that babies get burnt that babies get
burnt that babies get burnt that babies

get burnt that babies get burnt when
they bombs baghdad? that babies get burnt

that babies get burnt when they bombs
baghdad? when they bombs baghdad

when they bombs baghdad when they bombs
baghdad when they bombs

baghdad when they bombs baghdad when they bombs baghdad
when they bombs beirut when they bombs panama when they
bombs libya when they bombs hiroshima when they bombs cuba
when they bombs baghdad when they bombs biloxi when they
bombs birmingham when they bombs baghdad when they
bombs port au prince when they bombs bosnia when they
bombs soudan whan they bombs afghanistan when they bombs
baghdad when they bombs blackfeet. they bombed nagasaki…
don't ya'll know babies get burnt? when they bombs bpp whan
they bombs move phillie when they bombs vietnam when they
bombed vietnam when they bomb vietnam when they bombed
vietnam. did ya'll know babies get burnt? babies get burnt babies
get burnt babies get burnt babies get burnt babies get burnt
babies get burnt babies get burnt babies get burnt babies get
burnt babies get burnt babies get burnt babies
babies get…
when they bombs baghdad!?

those flags
(this is not a homophobe pome)

con   shit   tution   demo
crackershitstem
con   federate
confederate/federate
raise the tax rate   fed con   raise the flags at the
federal building
another southern capital building bombing?
republic   klan
getting done by the donkey and
elephants in this congress   i digress.
this is not a homophobe pome   these flags these
flags
those flagsthesefags   allthesameallthesameallthesame allthe-
sameallthesameallthesame insane and strangebedfellows. these flags
those fags they phallus fascist they faggit fascist   bundles
of sticks
politricks democrackers   republiklan wave they
white flags on sticks.
meaningless. flatulence.stars and bars and garters.   same 'ol
death certifikits
timestentimestwentyhowmany casualties? times ten times twenty
casualties.
 stealth panama bomber easier tool for lynchings.
opposed to secessionist stars and bars same as con
shit   tution
repub licks
signers on list.
fifty nifty united states there are 13 original colonies
these flags these flags those fags those flags those flags those
fallacious those facetious those phallus fascist faggits
strangebedfellows redneck house/palace these fags they flatulence

they foul those flags those fags.   same. all   the same.
                              all the same.
those fags they fascist mad cause you burned they
flags. stars and stripes   forever?
(blasted bastards)   stars and
bars on a niggah troop casket.
(this is not a homophobe pome)

nov. 5th 1996

(first of all) (fuck jesse helms) (today i voted)

i voted today. but felt no justice was made. but felt no
progression was made.

(for toils of khamets enslave[s]d.)   they gave me a sticker. said: i
voted today.
i voted today. de muck rat.   re pub lickin.
in(depends dent)

grandfather clause.   polltax (ill)(literacy test)
remained validated.
mama said backs had been bruised. mama said churchbombs.
people beaten
buried for this....   for this?   sticker: i voted today?
but still seemed unredeemed
runjesserunrunjesserunkeephopealivekeephopealiveupwithhope-
downwith
dope
concentration on a koon pre-diction. hymietown crucifixion.
ain't no fiction
(so called chosen frozen ....)

"he speaks so well"
colin cancer in lieu of a spitshine.
got a sticker.

said: i voted today!
and still no pickaninny presidents!?

barbershoptalk
(if i were prez.)another b pome

related at naps and paps barbershop somewhere off fayetteville st.
by awar jones beedy johnson:

i'm just a bill yes i'm only a bill and i'm sitting here on capitol hill....

if i were president, if i were president....

i would smoke blunts
in the oval office
w/ biiiches
(yes senator i did inhale)

in the cabinet with cubano cigarellos
and bang broads in the oval office
boardroom
break backs in the back
of airforce one's bathroom

bone baby girl interns
on the atom bomb control board
in the cockpit of the
stealth bomber
in berkeley. in barbados.
in great britain and bangor maine.
and kennebunkport
and boston   on top of the constitution

in PA.   and the bell tower with the liberty bell
ringing bells
in bangladesh. in brazil. in bosnia.
serving serbs. sydney. buttering buttocks

broads buns on the outback.
show ya'll who the baddest boy
like jim bakker.
i run the brawlingest country in the first world!

so tell FBICBSCIAABCPBSCSPANNBC
i ain't answering shit....
i'm the muphucking president!

(i believe bill would be a better baller if'n he were a brotha)

:said he at the checker table.

well i hope and pray that i will but today i am still just a bill.

good old amerikkkan boys pt. II

..two die in pearl,missisippi…three murdered in west paducah,kentucky..five
murdered, jonesboro,arkansas two killed in

smear the lambsblood above the doors.

there's a plot to kill the psychee of lil' negroe boys.
and **"good"** old amerikkan boys. in backwoods.
from 10-13 learn to shoot.
and they shoots to kill. and they shoots to kill
cause there aim is good.
with boyish **"good"** looks. mild mannered boy next door.
"good" old amerikkkan boys.
mild mannered **"good"** old amerikkklan boys.
in the amerikkkan public eye
hard to identify. **"good"** family backgrounds. amiable.
"good" student. well liked.
"good" students. and their aim is **"good"**.
arkansas/kentucky school houses.
and their aim
is **"good"**
but still there's a plot to kill the psychee of lil' negroe boys?
killing the psychee of lil' negroe boys.
remember scottsboro?

while **good** old amerikkkan boys kill.

springfield,oregon..in other news..littleton,colorado columbine highschool
students massacred copycat
killings…

dinesh d'souza dozens

dear dinesh,
i will not run the dozens on you in your insolent stupor. i will
not cut your blue blk./brwn. ass down off your caste rope/noose.
you so readily perpetuate not only for yourself but others to
hang from your neo-immigrant gallows. i realize colonialistic
indoaryanization can be a heavy thing (it really is!) but for you
and those other boozhee' brwn./ blueblk. academes that think
shit sweet…this is for you:

let's build ourselves a timemachine/with gears that whirr/and
windows clean/transport you back/way to the past/of racisms
begin/to contradict/your so-called racisms end/you new
immigrant east indien/have no concept of u.s. sins/of trail of
tears/ of middle pass./of conquistadores/and cowboy cast/of
abortion clinics/of nippon blast/of monroe doctrines expanse
vast/it's sickening to speak out of place/from comfort zone and
shielded space/let's land somewhere round '29/white
nationalisms/and jim crow signs/where crowds are frenzied/
lynch law exist/strangefruit flourish/in missisipp. mist/alleged
rape and ku klux task/i bet they'd lynch dinesh blk. ass.

greetings from cablinasia

....where oddly striped tigers become masters and sport green
jackets
and those poor bastards lost in the woods and jungles of a place
called thirdworld;
          anywhere~~~~~
have banquets catered by dennies. maincourse: collard greens
chicken & watermelon. table talk with tarzan and fuzzy zoeller.
sponsored by texaco. featuring musical guest mariah carey and
mike'blk. or wht.' jackson. we offer an exclusive cherry stained
set of poplarwood golfclubs
if you have reservations. if your a second class citizen i.e.
indianafricanasian
you will be denied   reservations. because you belong on
reservations.

welcome to the land of the nondescript. 3/4 of the formula
colonized. wartorn.
1/4 colonizer. maker of war.
no sirree buddy. no africans here.   who wants that
confusion?
who wants to be wholey african /   indian?
who needs that stress?
cause you can't be colonized...
and colonialist.
or is that
afrikan-columbian.
kristopher did discover this here...well didn't he?
greetings from cablinasia.   we
don't have an army. but if we did you could be all that you
could be

without actually   being   yourself?
no passport.   no visa.
no citizenship.
unless you are trying to hide   from   yourself?
like the brownbeigewhiteblackgrey spots   in camouflage
pattern.
can't hide you cause everyone sees yoo.
mymothermyfathergrandmasgrandpasgreatgrandpasgrandmasstep-
mothersfathersauntscousin.
was one qtr. malaysianfrenchfilipino3/8italiandominican-
mulatto3.5%puertoricangermanquadroon1/12octoroonjewishmest
izo2/7thshalfcastealaskanethiopian10.9ozs.shawneeaboriginehin-
ditwofourthsmoroccancherokeealbinomediterraneanapachemiddle
easternrussiannigerian5.8%irishindochinesearyanliberianjapanese-
hawaiianethnicazerbaijanian.
cullurds.
not easily held within the narrow scientific confines of
mendelian
mongoloidnegroidcaucasoid trinities. and surely darwin turns in
his grave
fore what percentage of the pheno/genotypes
are the fittest?...
surely the cablinasians!   checking box other does not
quantify on applications.
confusing to census of populations. cablinasians. proud to
reverse racism.
cause it is cancerous. and it has indeed taken on a new and even
deadlier tone. called ignorance or
ignorance of or the ignoring of

there ever being an existence of...

(let me finish)

brought into curriculum by multiculturalism. in which those that
are outside of the system. are burdened with the most vicious
forms of institutionalisms. institutionalized and practiced upon
the backs of...those institutionalized and practiced upon are now
so   called   purveyors   of~~~~
i'm glad i'm not blk. you see it's easier for me to hide behind the
mask..to hide behind the mask and consider hues and tones that
compose me. to identify bloodlines. while misidentifyingactual
problem. that's more convenient to seem as if i am not down
with you and all that you do.   but they know.
onedrop rule. 1/15th. 3/5ths a man. only since i can. i simply
ignore. close my door in utopia. cablinasia suburbia. i identify
by a check of the multiculti or multieth. box or simply check
other. scared someone will call me....

"what are you?"

dick nixon:a song i had writ in the smr. of 1969

(precedence dae)*

tricky dicky nixon you jerking me off
tricky dicky nixon you jerking me off
trick dick nixon you jerking me off jerking me off
jerking me off jerking me off.....
jimmy carter gerald ford
hey you jerked me off
reagan bush bill clinton
yeah you jerking me off
lbj jfk hey you jerking me off jerking me off
jerked me off jerking me off
now george washington jefferson jerked me off
ikeroosevelt and abie baby jerked me
(and it felt so good)
it's precedence dae how's it feel to get an executive handjob?
it feels good and it feels so good....tricky dicky nixon

* to Jb's funky watergate accompaniment

me & j. edgar hoover

(or the allowance of an (ill)legal (?) gov. agency to maintain
clandestine operations i.e. COINTELPRO in an attempt to
undermine negro liberation on the continent of n. amerikkka)

me and j. edgar hoover   (guitarlicks)
searching through the night   "
searching high and searching low   "
ending civil rights   "
phonetaps and wiretaps   "
    chase h. raps through the night
     another COIN maneuver
      me and edgar hoover
     lace garter belts and white

iiiijustwonnathankyoufalettinmebemicelfagin*
  (gtr. mve.ment)

*shouts out to sly and the family

grey ojay blanket

blame jonnie boy for playing a racecard of a deal longtime dealt.
when court is casino u.s. supreme atlantic city/nevada profiting
off of too much blackjack.

off the skin of blk.bk.   an intricate game of russian roulette.
hide beneath my blanket w/poems and pages. reflective histories.
where the wild things are. here. but more otherworldly than real.
from coast to coast overwhelmingly rejoiced.
why be surprise.

(you hide beneath the obscurity of your grey o.j. blanket)

of antiquity woven this societal fabric to hide the
truth forever shadowy.
shadowing victimless crimes. guiltless accusers. timeless possessors.
criminality behind crooked pointing index. but five point back.
commonality and you without guilt or sin have not a
smooth stone to cast.
(hope you don't have mirrored ceilings)

profiteers mocking court system. arbitrary juror
pool hinged on curved bell.
i feel your quotients subliminals intelligent.

don't get me wrong (but phuck orenthal)   (he your product)

and somehow can't help but think your visualization
of vigilantism
stretches round   all   spook throat.

knowledgemints

jehovahjahallah.egungun.momsforinadvertentlyinspiringmetobeastar
vingartistbyexposingmetotheARTs.mypsychadelicbeginningsmy-
funkadelicnurturingsmygroovadelicblossomingsmyspurmadelicofferin
gs.thomIfortheearlierciphesdrums&kalimbas.).CVMH/spurmban-
quevetsvernstar&bashir(aboyandhisjockstrap?).schoollyjay.tonya"youa
preacher,preach"&monielove"iknowyougotsumthin'toreadtonite!"im
petusformyfirstreadingsatthenegrocollegeunionnest.expresso'-
selfandthecatfromcanadaconvenientlyuncullurd.ayeje"thesearemythig
hs".jeffshep&cosmiccantinaspoeticsoulloungewherewedon't-
clapwe_______.toothpick&thesmr.98catsthatlacedmyfeature.skinnyjinn
y.c.clark,esq"yo,bumrushtheshow"beneficent.mattsherm&thecypherc
rew(preciatethehostgig)..headzmag&98lb.angrielil'boiehelpinghone-
myhostingw/verbalkombat.marcella"youneedtohaveyourownt.v.show".
7min.screamingbillwitherslookingkdub&theroachzombeehouse.maraj
eb.yvette..biggestshoutsgotoPM7100/66AVandthemarylouwilliamsce
nterthirdshiftcrew(whoknew?).maureencullins(icheckedyes).scipoet&
haytiheritagecenter.bros.w/vision.infinitythecollective:ajubajoycher-
rylfloydteju.jazzpoetssociety.vibekhameleons:mofotee"i'mfrombrookl
yn/darkprince"kay,"boricacid"mums(inaironmonkeystylee).olufunke
&sonyahaynesstonesenter.naderaspr.99sautimpyahookup.reneeA.forth
etrailblaze.wellstower¢erfordocumentarystudies.exumbra99.kam
eka(resonancearetha).themaB.(wearthatorange,youworthy).returnof"f
uckpoems&theyareuseful"joelouis,jr.jaysullivan.eric(forthefrancesca-
convos).B&Nforthefreereads.johnwilliams(slamdudunnadudunna).my
babymumaterri(thankyouforO.).myfirdousi(soulwurds).torkwase.wire
grass.monchinski(inabout4secs.theteacherwillbegintospeak)UrbAbsgr
ooveallegiance(diallolives).codycods.markwellstrio.stevehobbstrio.the
originalbrownhornetbillcosbyphatalbertjunkyardband.mr.harry,Jr.fort
helinkwords.rev.wimp.beaforunspokenwords.elvinforspokenword.bay
bro.jermainecanphumk.webstersthirdnewinternationaldic-
tionaryunabridged.mrs.eaton.mrs.hartwell.mrs.buker.&allthathavespo
nsoredorin/directlyinfluencedmyphilology.dre'leongrayforthevisu-
alvodoun.sistuhfrances(let'sdefectdefacto).&lastbutnotleastshadrachme
shachabednego(yougonebelikebarrygordyupinthiscampcat).toallery-
bodybigshiloams.hollerback.yebeshia.

eyeseen

i see
eyesight
eye see
i have seen
eye seed
i scene   eyesite

aye...   seen?
see it   unseen
aye!   seen.
(have you seen)
i'se seen
seen i   essene
(sinaicyanide)
i think eye seen?
my eyes have seen
eyes sore   eye sore
my eye has seen the glory of the coming of
the lord?
eye soar